Materials

their Properties and Uses

David Byrne

Acknowledgements

Photos
Chris Honeywell, front cover, back cover, title page, contents page, pages 4, 5, 6 middle and bottom, 7, 9, 10 middle, 11, 13 main, 14 top, 15 main, 17, 19 and 20. Trip/R. Drury, page 6 top left. FLPA/Silvestris, page 6 top right. George Bernard/Science Photo Library, page 10 top left. Planet Earth Pictures/Ken Lucas, page 10 top right. Trevor Clifford, pages 13 top and 21 bottom. Tony Stone Images/Roger Markham Smith, page 15 inset top. Tony Stone Images/Baron Wolman, page 15 inset middle. Panos Pictures/Neil Cooper, page 16 top. Silvestris/Heiner Heine, page 16 middle. Trip/H. Rogers, page 16 bottom. Zefa/CPA, page 21 top

Illustrations
All illustrations by Oxford Illustrators.

Heinemann Educational Publishers
Halley Court, Jordan Hill, Oxford OX2 8EJ
a division of Reed Educational & Professional Publishing Ltd

OXFORD   MELBOURNE   AUCKLAND
JOHANNESBURG   BLANTYRE   GABORONE
IBADAN   PORTSMOUTH (NH) USA   CHICAGO

© Reed Educational & Professional Publishing Ltd 1997

First published 1997

02 01 00 99 98

10 9 8 7 6 5

British Library Cataloguing in Publication Data
A catalogue record for this book is available from the British Library.

ISBN 0 435 09568 4   *Materials: their Properties and Uses*
individual copy pack: 6 copies of 1 title

ISBN 0 435 09416 5   Stage F pack: 1 each of 7 titles

Colour reproduction by Reacta Graphics.

Printed and bound in Great Britain by Scotprint.

Contents

Types of materials

There are many different types of materials. The things we use every day are made from different materials. Do you know what materials these things are made from?

Some materials come from things that grow around us, or under the ground. These are called natural materials. Other materials are made by people. These are called man-made materials.

Wood

Wood is a natural material. There are two types of wood. Softwood is made from evergreen trees. Hardwood is made from trees that lose their leaves.

softwood forest

hardwood forest

Trees are cut down and cut into planks. The planks are dried. This is called seasoning.

Some wood is made from lots of very small pieces of wood pressed together. This type of wood is very hard and heavy.

Wood

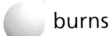 burns

is not magnetic

does not conduct electricity

absorbs liquid

Wood is used to make

furniture

musical instruments

paper

charcoal for barbecues

Paper

Paper is a man-made material. Most paper is made from wood. The wood is broken into chips. The chips are mixed with water and chemicals to make pulp.

The pulp is spread onto a moving belt. The belt carries the pulp through large rollers. The rollers squeeze the water out.

Hot rollers dry the paper. The paper is made into large rolls.

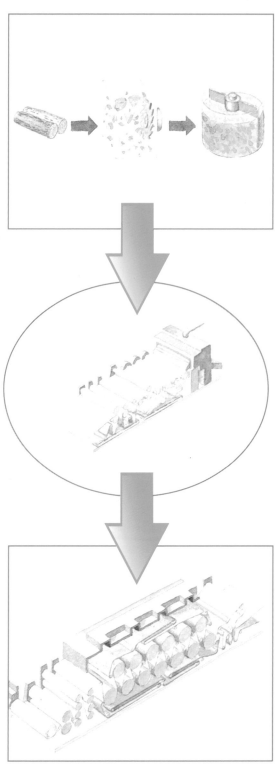

Paper

- burns
- is not magnetic
- does not conduct electricity
- absorbs liquid

Paper is used to make

- books and newspapers
- tissues
- cards
- boxes and sweet wrappers

Metal

Some metals are natural materials. These metals are found in the ground, like gold and silver.

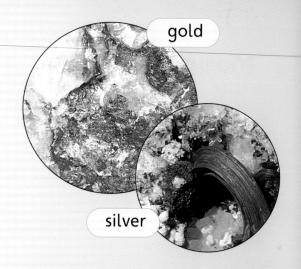
gold

silver

Some natural metals are found in rocks. The most common ones are aluminium and iron. Mines are dug to take the metals out of the ground.

Some metals are man-made materials. These are made when natural metals are mixed together. This new metal is called an alloy.

Metal

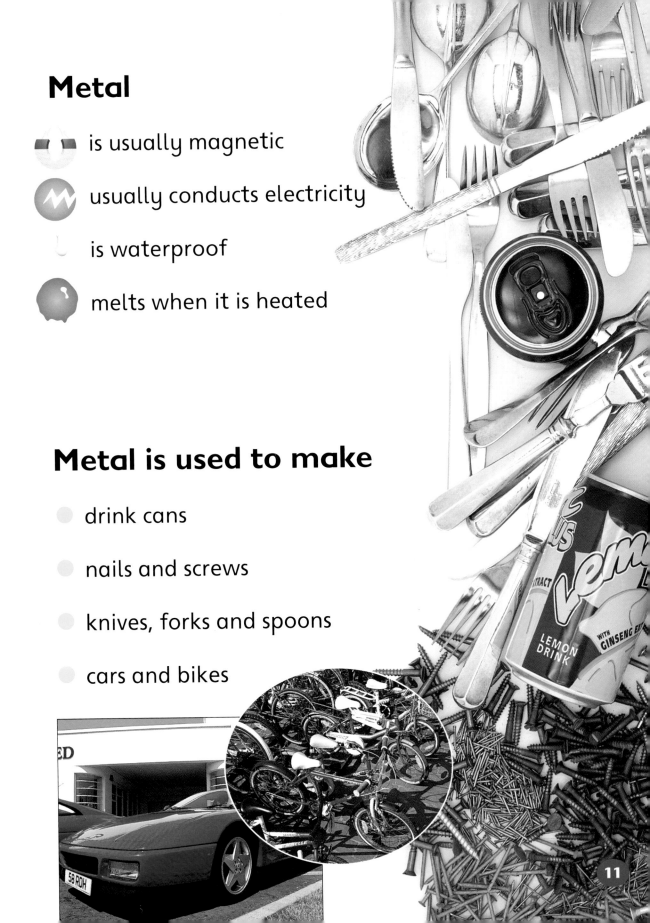

- is usually magnetic

- usually conducts electricity

- is waterproof

- melts when it is heated

Metal is used to make

- drink cans

- nails and screws

- knives, forks and spoons

- cars and bikes

Glass

Glass is a man-made material. It is made by heating sand and chemicals together.

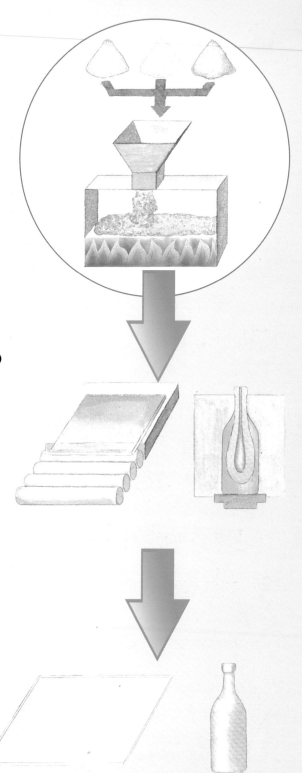

Glass can be melted into a liquid form. The liquid glass can be made into many shapes. It can be shaped by putting it into a mould. It can be shaped by spreading it into a flat sheet.

As the glass cools, it hardens and sets.

Glass

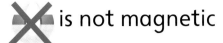 is not magnetic

is usually transparent

is waterproof

melts when it is heated

Glass is used to make

- bottles and containers

- lenses in glasses, telescopes and microscopes

- light bulbs

- windows

Plastic

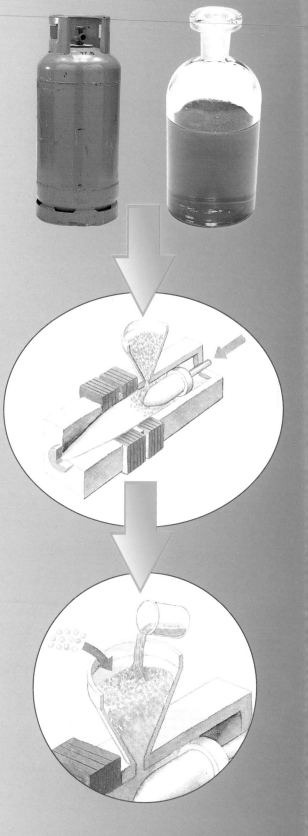

Plastic is a man-made material. It is made in a factory by heating chemicals together.

Some chemicals make soft plastic. The plastic can be made into shapes in a machine. Some chemicals make hard plastic. This can be used to make boats and aircraft.

Coloured dye can be added to the chemicals.

Plastic

 is not magnetic

 does not conduct electricity

is waterproof

 sometimes melts when it is heated

Plastic is used to make

- containers and plastic bags

- waterproof clothes

- toys

- boats and aircraft

Clay

Clay is a natural material. It is taken from the ground.

Clay can be made into many shapes. A potter can shape it using a special wheel.

Clay gets very hard if it is heated in a kiln or oven. This process is called firing. Clay is glazed and fired to make it strong.

Clay

 is not magnetic

 does not conduct electricity

 absorbs liquid if it is not fired

is waterproof if it is fired

Clay is used to make

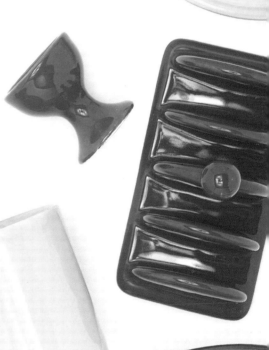

- plates, cups and bowls

- jewellery

- bricks

- tiles for walls and floors

Cement

Cement is a man-made material. It is made by heating clay and chalk together.

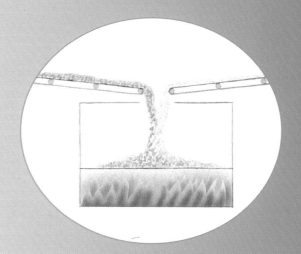

Sand, gravel and water are mixed with cement to make concrete. Concrete is used to make paths and roads.

Sand and water are mixed with cement to make mortar. Mortar holds bricks together. The bricks in houses are held together with mortar.

Cement

X is not magnetic

X does not conduct electricity

absorbs liquid

gets very hard when it is mixed with water and left to dry

Cement is used to make

- concrete for paths and roads

- mortar to hold bricks together

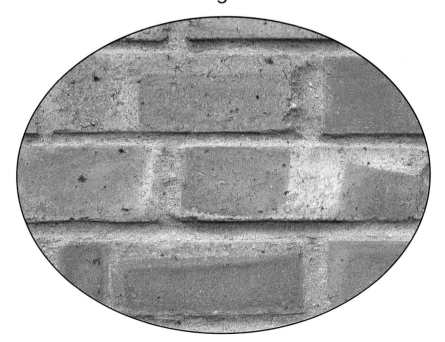

Save our resources

Every day we throw rubbish away. The rubbish that we throw away can cause pollution and make our environment untidy.

A lot of rubbish can be used again. Aluminium and steel cans, glass bottles, plastic containers and paper can all be recycled.

Special factories recycle different materials.

Metals are melted and used to make drink cans. Glass is melted down and used to make bottles. Old plastic bottles are used to make warm clothes. Paper is made into pulp and used to make greetings cards.

You can help by starting your own collection of materials for recycling.

Materials and their properties

Materials \ Properties	burns	magnetic	conducts electricity
wood			
paper			
metal			
glass			
plastic			
clay			
cement			

transparent	absorbs liquid	waterproof	melts when heated	gets hard when mixed with water

Index